Choices & Changes
IN LIFE, SCHOOL, AND WORK
Grade 5–6
Student Journal

National Council on Economic Education

*This publication was made possible through funding of the
Calvin K. Kazanjian Economics Foundation.*

Copyright © 2001, National Council on Economic Education, 1140 Avenue of the Americas, New York, NY 10036. All rights reserved. Some materials in this publication were previously published in *Choices & Changes,* copyright © 1992 by the National Council on Economic Education. No part of this book may be reproduced in any form or by any means without written permission of the publisher. Printed in the United States of America.

ISBN 1-56183-583-8   5 4 3 2 1

Mind Map

To do the things that you want to do, you can develop your human capital (skills and knowledge). Create a mind map that illustrates the human capital you have which helps you accomplish the things you want to do. Place your name in the center of the paper, e.g., **Kimberly's Human Capital (Skills and Knowledge)**.

Your mind map should include:

- Ten skills or important things that you now know how to do.
- Three things that you would like to be able to do in the future.
- Five skills or pieces of knowledge that you must learn to be able to do the things you want to do in the future.

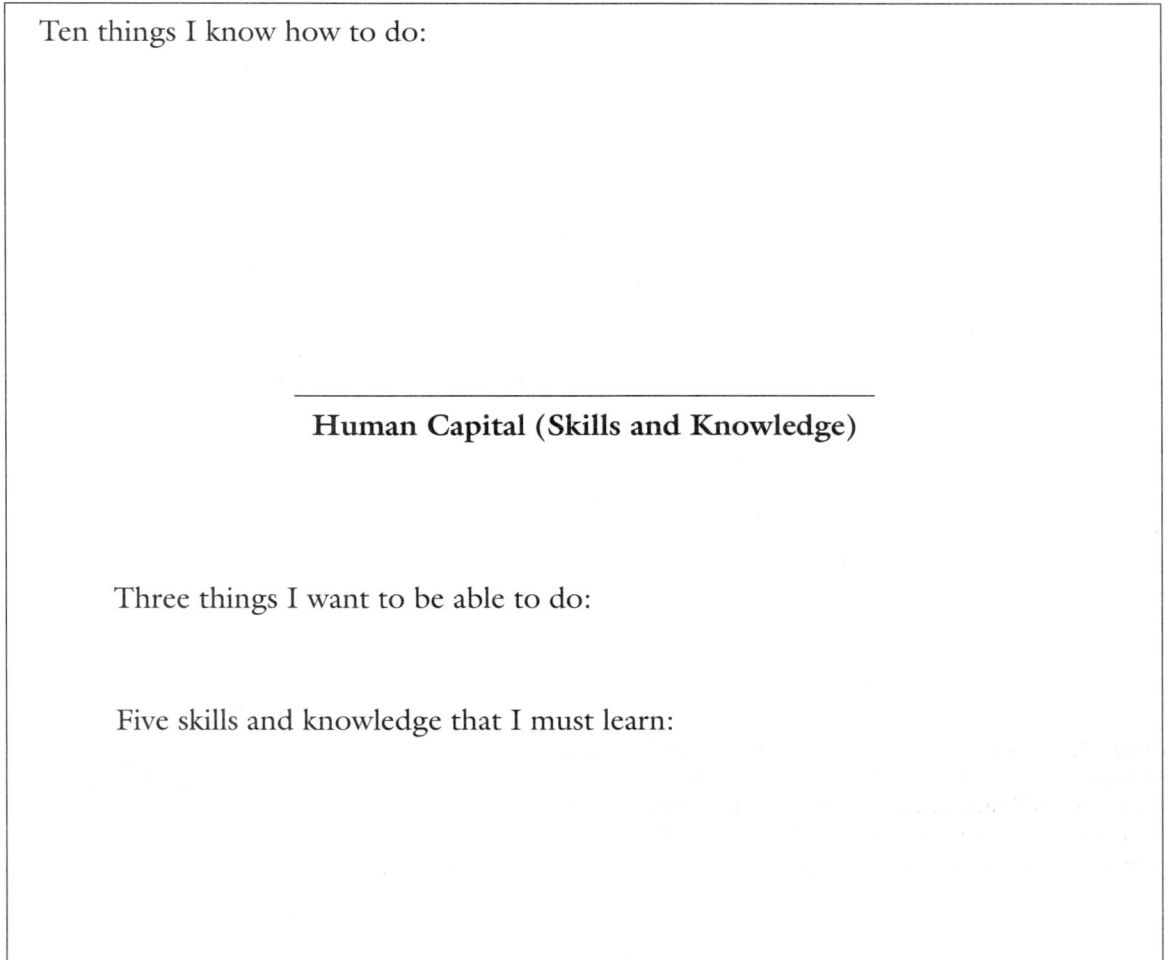

The Navigation School at Sagres

In the early 1400s, the rulers of England, France, and Portugal envied the wealth of Venice and Genoa. Trade with Asia and Africa was the reason for their great wealth. The land routes to Asia and Africa were long and dangerous. If water routes could be found, then the rulers of England, France, and Portugal could be wealthier and more powerful.

The king of Portugal was very interested in finding a water route to Africa and Asia. The Portuguese were sea-going people and knew much about sea travel. Even so, the most experienced sailors were afraid of sailing into strange waters. They feared shipwrecks or being blown off course.

Prince Henry, the leader of Portugal, was determined to find a water route to Asia and Africa. He knew that before sailors would take long voyages, they needed tools that would get them home safely and a ship that could be steered easily. Henry created a school of navigation at Sagres (SAH-greesh) in southern Portugal. The potential rewards of finding a water route to Asia were great, so everything learned at Sagres was kept top secret.

Prince Henry gathered a library of books and maps. Then he hired navigators, mathematicians, cartographers, geographers, astronomers, and sea captains to be teachers. These specialists taught the Portuguese sailors everything they knew about navigation and reading maps.

While studying at Sagres, sailors learned to use a triangular quadrant and magnetic compass to find direction. They measured latitude by turning the pointer on the astrolabe (AS-truh-layb). They learned to measure the angle of the horizon in relation to the North Star by using a cross-staff. Longitude was measured by calculating how far and how long they traveled.

The development of the rudder allowed shipbuilders to build a new kind of ship, the caravel. A caravel was steered without a large crew of oarsmen and was faster and easier to navigate. It carried two kinds of sails, a square sail and a triangular lateen sail. The caravel could sail into the wind as well as with the wind. The caravel could turn around and come home no matter which way the wind blew.

2-1 (continued)

The Navigation School at Sagres

The development of the caravel and new knowledge to use navigation tools gave Prince Henry's crews the confidence they needed to sail far from Portugal.

Prince Henry's school of navigation made it possible for future sea captains and explorers to travel farther and to safely reach Asia and Africa. The school made it possible for sailors to navigate more accurately. Developing new technology and learning to use navigation tools opened a great era of exploration.

The rulers of countries who were willing to take the risks of finding a water route to the goods of Asia and Africa became wealthy.

2-2

I Am a Teacher at Sagres

You are a teacher at Sagres. Your job is to teach Prince Henry's sailors. You will make a presentation to the class, imagining that they are sailors.

Option 1
- **Choose** one of the tools used at the school of navigation: the magnetic compass, triangular quadrant, cross-staff, or astrolabe.
- **Research** how the tool helped sailors navigate their caravel. What will you have to learn to successfully teach the sailors? Perhaps you will have to turn to others who have written books or authored information on the Internet, or find an expert to teach you.
- **Construct** a model of the tool or draw a poster-size picture to use as you teach.
- **Present** what you have learned.

Option 2
- **Research** how the caravel was built and maneuvered.
- **Construct** a two- or three-dimensional model of a caravel ship.
- **Present** what you have learned. Be sure to explain how the caravel made sea travel easier and safer.

Your class presentation will be evaluated on the following criteria:

Scoring Rubric for the Class Presentation				
Criteria \ Score	Highly evident (4)	Frequently evident (3)	Somewhat evident (2)	Not evident (1)
The information presented was accurate.				
A model or visual was used in the presentation.				
The presentation was well organized and easy to understand.				
The presentation was interesting and kept the audience's attention.				

What Is It Worth?
Data

The United States Bureau of the Census collects information about people in the United States. This information is available for analysis. Have you thought about your future learning and earning? By graphing the data in the table, you will see what producers are paying for human capital based on the following education levels. These income averages are for adults, 25 years of age and older.

Directions:

1. Compare the average incomes of males and females with the same education level.

2. Round each income to the nearest thousand. This will make the income data easier to graph on the next journal page.

Education Level and Income in the United States, 1998

Highest Education Level	Males Actual	Males Rounded	Females Actual	Females Rounded
Less than 9th grade	$12,571	$13,000	$7,914	$8,000
9th to 12th grade (no diploma)	$17,462	_____	$9,582	_____
High School Graduate (diploma, GED)	$26,542	_____	$13,786	_____
Some College (no degree)	$31,627	_____	$18,445	_____
Associate Degree (junior college, AA)	$35,962	_____	$21,290	_____
Bachelor's Degree (BA, BS)	$45,749	_____	$27,415	_____
Master's Degree (MA, MS, MBA)	$55,784	_____	$36,888	_____
Doctorate Degree (Ph.D, Ed.D)	$65,319	_____	$46,275	_____
Professional Degree (MD, DDS, DVM, JD)	$76,362	_____	$43,490	_____

What Is it Worth?
Graph

1. Label the vertical axis of the graph: **Income.**

   Label each line of the vertical axis. Use increments of $5,000.

   Begin with $0, $5,000, $10,000, $15,000, etc.

2. Label the horizontal axis of the graph: **Highest Education Level**.

   Label two bars with an education level, the lower level on the right side and the higher level on the left side.

3. Select two different colored pencils.

   Choose one color to represent **Females.**

   Choose another color to represent **Males**.

   Color the graph key.

4. Use the rounded income figures from *Student Journal,* page 3-1 to make a double bar graph.

5. Write a title for the graph.

What Is It Worth?
Graph

Graph Key

Males ☐   Females ☐

Graph Title _____

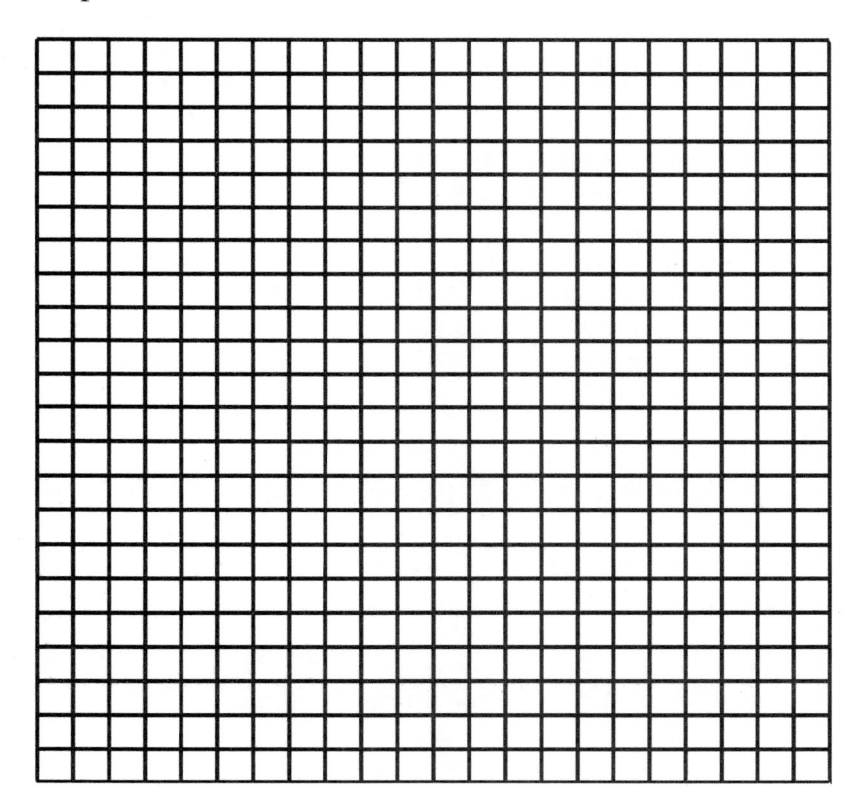

What Is It Worth?
Questions

Answer the following questions about your completed graph from *Student Journal* 3-2, page 2.

1. Explain the cause of increasing income as shown on the double bar graph.

   _____
   _____
   _____

2. What are the differences in average incomes between people who have some high school education, but no high school diploma and high school graduates?

   _____
   _____

3. Have you thought about your future goals? How much education do you need to reach your career goals?

   _____
   _____
   _____

4. What results when people improve their human capital?

   _____
   _____

UNIT ONE ASSESSMENT 1

Home and Community Education Survey

Directions

1. Identify ten working adults you know who are family members or friends, 25 years old or older. Do not ask more than one teacher.
2. Ask each adult to identify his or her highest level of education, using the levels listed below.
3. Tally your results on the chart below.
4. These results will be combined with those of the rest of the class on the next page.

Highest Education Level	Males	Females
Less than 9th grade		
9th to 12th grade (no diploma)		
High School Graduate/GED		
Some College (no degree)		
Associate Degree (junior college/AA)		
Bachelor's Degree (BA/BS)		
Master's Degree (MA/MS/MBA)		
Doctorate Degree (PhD/EdD)		
Professional Degree (MD/JD/DDS/DVM)		

*There is no scarcity of opportunity to make a living at what you love;
there's only a scarcity of resolve.*

Wayne Dyer

UNIT ONE ASSESSMENT 2

Home and Community Education Survey Comparison

Directions

1. Combine the individual surveys from the previous page into one classroom total. Put the classroom totals on this chart in the number column. Total each column (male and female).
2. Use a calculator to find the percentages of males and females at each education level.
3. Compare the percentages from your data to the 1998 U.S. Census data below.

Total Education Levels in Our Class

Highest Education Level	Male Number	Male Percent	Female Number	Female Percent
Less than 9th grade				
9th to 12th grade (no diploma)				
High School Diploma/GED				
Some College (no degree)				
Associate Degree (junior college/AA)				
Bachelor's Degree (BA/BS)				
Master's Degree (MA/MS/MBA)				
Doctorate Degree (PhD/EdD)				
Professional Degree (MD/DDS)				
Total				

Total Education Levels in the United States, 1998**

Highest Education Level	Male Number	Male Percent	Female Number	Female Percent
Less than 9th grade	5,641,000	7%	5,419,000	6%
9th to 12th grade (no diploma)	7,366,000	9%	7,559,000	9%
High School Graduate	25,636,000	32%	29,330,000	35%
Some College (no degree)	13,935,000	17%	15,173,000	18%
Associate Degree (AA)	5,766,000	7%	6,931,000	8%
Bachelor's Degree (BA/BS)	14,614,000	18%	14,218,000	17%
Master's Degree (MA/MS/MBA)	4,772,000	6%	4,837,000	6%
Doctorate Degree (PhD/EdD)	1,443,000	2%	567,000	1%
Professional Degree (MD, JD, DVM)	1,695,000	2%	788,000	1%
Total	80,868,000	100%*	84,844,000	100%*

* Due to rounding, the total does not equal 100%.
** U.S. Census Bureau, "Historical Income Tables - People," Table P-16, 1998. www.census.gov/hhes/income/histinc/p16.html

Seth and Mary's Dilemma

James Holcomb and his family lived comfortably on the land given to James when his father died in 1737. Their farm was not far from London. It had a small stream, a garden area, and grazing land for a few cattle. James and his three sons worked the land, producing enough to feed and clothe the family. There was a little money left each month to purchase a few other goods.

When their daughter, Anne, married George Logan, she moved to the Logan home. When sons James Jr., William, and Seth married, their new wives came to live with them on the Holcomb farm. Within a few years, each of the new families grew as children were born. The house seemed smaller, and the farm could not produce enough to keep all the family members comfortable.

In December of 1762, James Sr. became very ill and died of pneumonia. Following the English tradition of primogeniture, the eldest son, James Jr., inherited the land and his father's property. James Jr.'s mother, Sarah, would stay at the home, living with James and his wife and children.

When James Sr. died, some of the Holcomb land was sold to pay taxes. The remaining land could not support the three growing families.

William, the second-oldest son, became an apprentice to Patrick Cosgrove, a shoemaker; Cosgrove owed a favor to James Sr. The youngest son, Seth, faced a dilemma. He and his wife Mary had three children. He received no family land and he had little money to buy land. He only knew how to farm, but he had five mouths to feed. What would he do?

One day as Seth and Mary walked through London, they saw a notice about land in the North American colonies. This free land was for those brave enough to travel across the ocean and stake a claim in the wilderness west of Virginia.

Seth and Mary thought that with the small amount of money they had saved and a small loan from brother James, their family could begin a new life farming in the colonies. They thought about the reasons to go to the colonies and the reasons to stay in England.

4-1 (continued)

Seth and Mary's Dilemma

Reasons to stay in England

- Close to family and friends
- The cost of travel on a ship
- A long and dangerous journey
- Unknown problems in a new land

Reasons to emigrate to the colonies

- Cheap land to clear and farm west of the Virginia Colony
- No need to develop new skills—Seth already knew how to farm
- Opportunity for Seth's children to own their own land
- No taxes to pay to the king

4-2

Virginia Colony Land Advertisement

Nova Britannia,

OFFERING MOST

Excellent fruites by Planting in

VIRGINIA.

Exciting all such as be well-affected
To further the fame

London

Printed for Samuel Macham, and are to befold at
His Shop in Pauls Church-yard, at the
Signe of the Bul-head
1763

Use a map and scale to find the distance from London, England to Richmond, Virginia.

_____ miles

What risks do you think Seth and Mary will face as they travel this distance?

_____
_____
_____

Benefits and Costs of Immigrating to the Colonies

Use the information in *Student Journal*, page 4-1: *Seth and Mary's Dilemma*.

1. Discuss with your group the costs or risks of deciding to emigrate to North America. List the costs in the "costs" column.
2. Discuss the benefits of deciding to emigrate. List the benefits in the "benefits" column.

COSTS	BENEFITS

Should Seth and Mary emigrate to the colonies? Why or why not?

_____
_____
_____

4-4

The Proclamation of 1763

Seth and Mary decided to travel to the colonies. They planned to settle in the territory west of the Virginia Colony. The family prepared their belongings for the long trip. They would not be able to take much, so they chose carefully: Clothing, cooking supplies, farming tools, and one toy for each of the children. Seth and Mary knew that it would be difficult, but the free land west of Virginia offered an opportunity that they would not have in England.

When the time of their voyage was just a few months away, Seth heard about a proclamation, an order signed by King George. It was October 7, 1763. The royal proclamation ordered that from that day on, there could be no settlements on the lands west of the Appalachian Mountains. King George reserved that land for the Indians who helped Britain win the Seven Years War against France. Now Seth and Mary faced another very difficult decision. They had to consider their new benefits and their new costs.

What were Seth and Mary's alternatives?

- Stay in England. Seth might be able to find work in the city, but the family would have no place to live and few prospects for a good life.

- Go to the colonies to start a farm in the West. They could go to the colonies and take their chances by settling on Indian land despite the King's orders. This option would subject them to a risk of prison or trouble with the Native Americans.

- Seth could sign an indenture to go to Virginia and work to earn 50 acres of land; the family could join him several years later. An indenture was a contract. An indentured servant was a person who agreed to provide five to seven years of unpaid labor in return for free passage across the ocean, food, clothing, and shelter.

- Did they have any other alternatives?

A journey of a thousand miles begins with a single step.
Chinese Proverb

4-5

Steps for Decision Making

A. Clarify the alternatives.
   Are there additional alternatives?
   - Stay in England
   - Apprentice with Mr. Smith
   - Move to the frontier
   - Other ?

B. Identify the criteria Seth and Mary should consider.
   Clearly define each criterion.
   - Economic opportunity
   - Risk of death or prison
   - Money costs
   - Consequences for the family
   - Freedom
   - Other ?

C. Evaluate each alternative according to each of the criteria.
   Use a system of (+) , (?), or (-) to evaluate each alternative.

D. Analyze the results of the evaluation.

E. Draw a conclusion about the best alternative.

F. Make a decision.

History has demonstrated that the most notable winners usually encountered heartbreaking obstacles before they triumphed. They won because they refused to become discouraged by their defeats.

Bertie C. Forbes

4-6

Seth and Mary's Decision

Use the steps for decision making.

1. List the alternatives on the left.
2. List the criteria across the top.
3. Evaluate each alternative according to the criteria.

> Evaluate each alternative as:
> + = Greater benefit than cost
> ? = Equal or questionable benefit and cost
> − = Greater cost than benefit

CRITERIA / ALTERNATIVE	Freedom	Risk	Money Cost	Effects on the family	Economic opportunity
STAY IN ENGLAND					
SIGN AN INDENTURE					
FARM IN THE WEST					
_____					

4. Analyze the results.
5. What alternative should Seth and Mary choose? _____

Why? _____

_____

_____

4-7

My Future Decision

My problem or goal is:

_____

My alternatives are:

1. _____   2. _____

3. _____   4. _____

My criteria are:

1. _____   2. _____

3. _____   4. _____

5. _____

Evaluate each alternative as: + = Greater benefit than cost.
                                               ? = Equal or questionable benefit.
                                               − = Greater cost than benefit.

CRITERIA / ALTERNATIVE					

My decision is _____

because _____

From *Choices and Changes in Life, School, and Work*, 5–6, © National Council on Economic Education, New York, NY

5-1

Human Capital for Production

Product #1: 2" × 2" squares, ¼" thick

Human Capital

Product #2: Cube

Improved Human Capital

Product #3: Tower

Improved Human Capital

Product #4:

Improved Human Capital

Sculpture

From *Choices and Changes in Life, School, and Work*, 5–6, © National Council on Economic Education, New York, NY

The Circular Flow Model

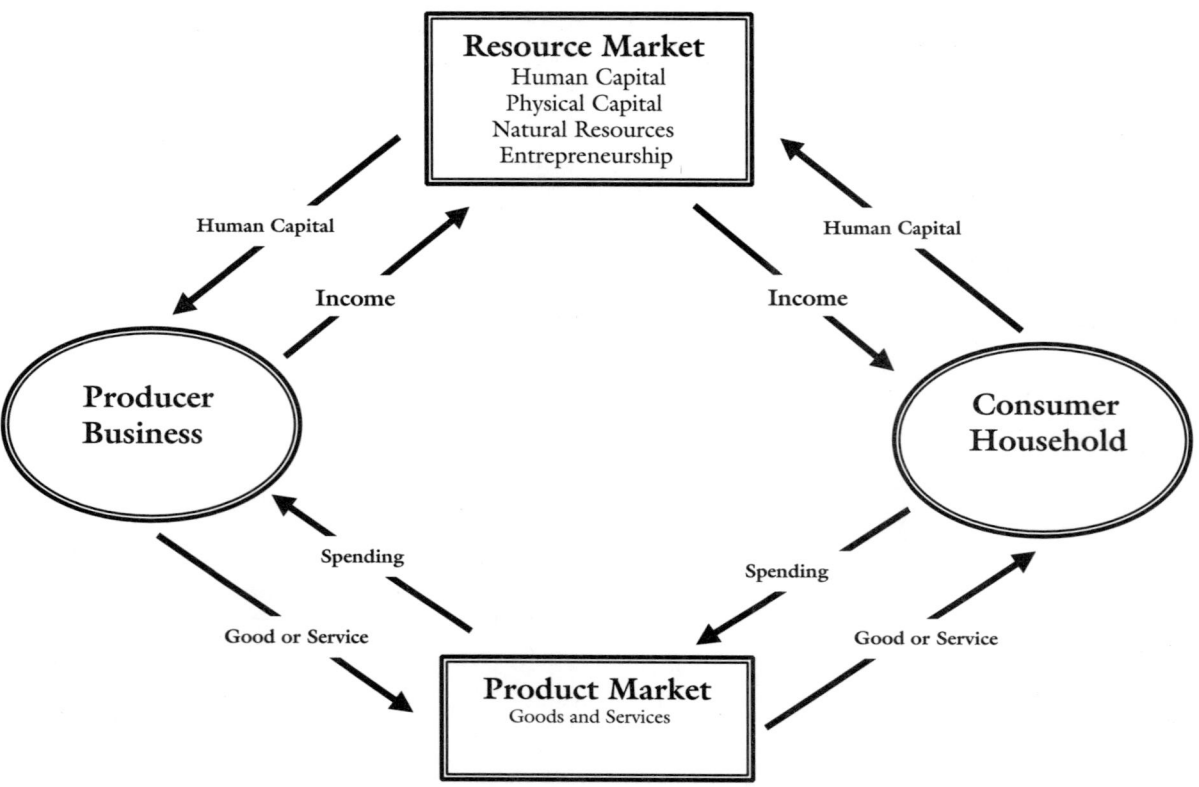

Businesses that grow by development and improvement do not die. But when a business ceases to be creative, when it believes it has reached perfection and needs to do nothing but produce—no improvement, no development—it is done.

Henry Ford

6-2

Consumer Tally Sheet

Income	Consumer Spending

Producer Tally Sheet

Resources Purchased	Goods or Services Sold

Successful men keep moving. They make mistakes, but they don't quit.
Conrad Hilton

6-3

Understanding the Circular Flow Model

Directions. Fill in the blanks with the labels of the sectors, markets, and flows of the Circular Flow Model.
Labels to use: income, spending, goods or services, human capital, resource market, product market, producer, consumer. Hint: A label may be used more than one time.

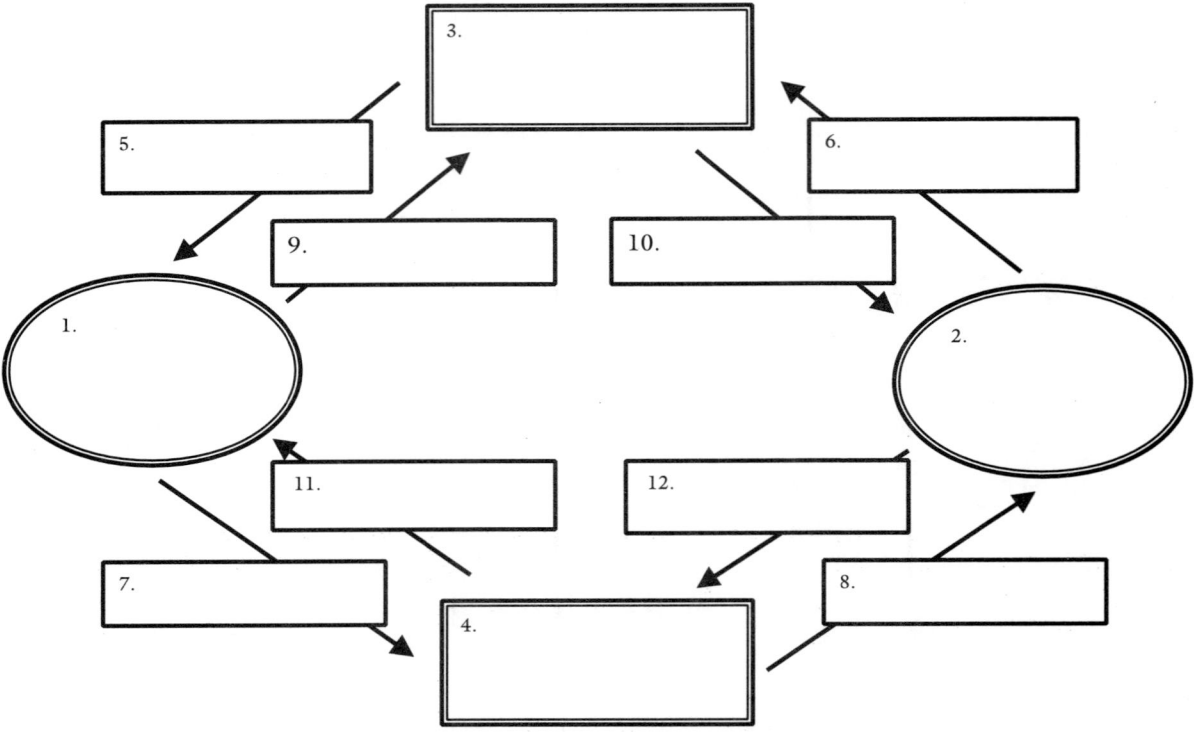

It takes less time to do things right than to explain why you did it wrong.
Henry Wadsworth Longfellow

6-4

Circular Flow Riddle

Riddle: I am a four letter word that fits in each of the blanks in the following sentences.

Who am I? _____   _____   _____   _____

Directions

Write the correct word in each of the blanks.

When people have _____ human capital resources to sell, they can earn _____ income.

When consumers earn _____ income, they can buy _____ goods and services.

When consumers want to buy _____ goods and services, producers will buy _____ human capital resources.

When producers buy _____ human capital resources, people earn _____ income.

We keep moving forward, opening up new doors, and doing new things, because we're curious and curiosity keeps leading us down new paths.
                                                            Walt Disney

From *Choices and Changes in Life, School, and Work*, 5–6, © National Council on Economic Education, New York, NY

UNIT TWO ASSESSMENT

Decision-Making Organizer

You make decisions every day. Some decisions are easy and other decisions are more difficult. The difficult decisions usually involve greater risks. Those decisions are best made by thinking in advance about the benefits and costs of the alternatives.

1. Choose a situation.
    - **1492** Should King Ferdinand and Queen Isabella pay for Columbus' voyage?
    - **1776** Should I remain loyal to King George or become a patriot and rebel?
    - **1852** Should my family follow the Oregon Trail and move to the west?
    - **1863** Should President Lincoln issue the Emancipation Proclamation?
    - **1882** Should we limit the number of immigrants to the United States?
    - **1945** Should the United States drop the atomic bomb on Japan?
    - **1964** Should the United States increase its involvement in Vietnam?
    - **2002** Should the driving age be increased to 18?
    - **2002** Should the United States abolish the Electoral College system?
2. Research additional information about the question and the time of the decision.
3. Complete the *Decision-Making Organizer*.

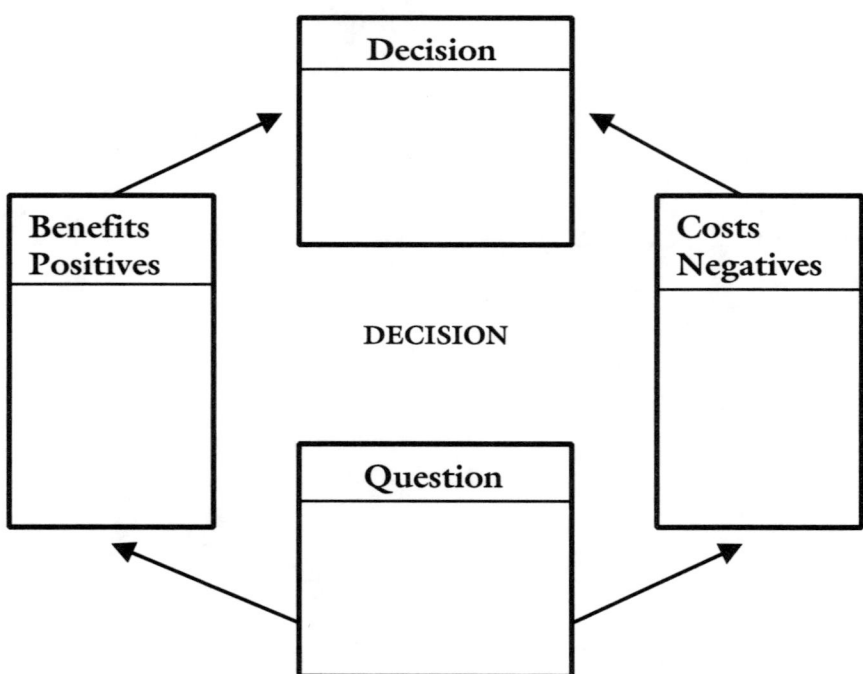

24 From *Choices and Changes in Life, School, and Work*, 5–6, © National Council on Economic Education, New York, NY

7-1

I Can Produce Something People Want

1. My product is called _____

2. To make my product, the productive resources I used were _____
_____
_____

3. To make my product, the human capital I used was _____
_____

4. My product will be wanted by _____
_____

5. Consumers will use my product to _____
_____

My product looks like

Story Map

Characters _____

_____

Setting
(time and place) _____

_____

Problem _____

_____

_____

Plot
(events) _____

_____

_____

_____

_____

Resolution _____

_____

_____

Consumer Wants Derive Demand for Resources

Directions. Complete the derived demand wheel. For each peanut product, identify one human capital resource, one physical capital resource, and one natural resource that is required to produce the product. For example, a Snickers candy bar requires chocolate (natural), a pot in which to melt the chocolate (physical capital), and a designer (human capital) to design the wrapper.

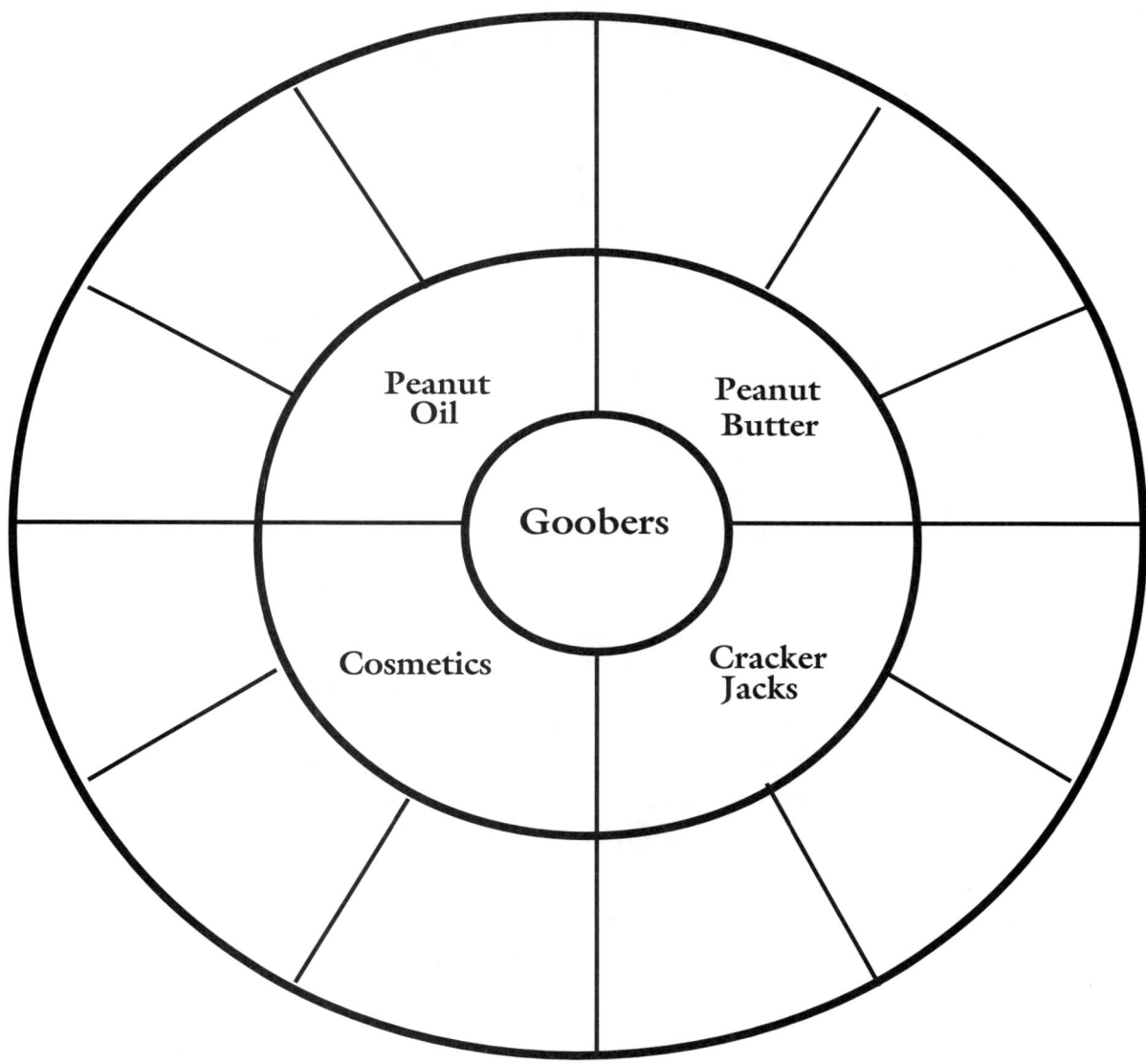

7-4

Peanut Products Created by George Washington Carver

cheese	milk
coffee	flour
ink	dyes
plastics	wood stains
soap	linoleum
medicinal	cosmetics
plastics	synthetic rubber
shaving cream	paper

"It is not the style of clothes one wears, neither the kind of automobile one drives, nor the amount of money one has in the bank, that counts. These mean nothing. It is simply service that measures success."

George Washington Carver

Star Company Production Report

Star Production Resource Costs

Paper (variable cost)	$5.00	Scissors (fixed cost)	$100.00
Human Capital (variable cost)	$5.00	Tables/Chairs (fixed cost)	$100.00
		Patterns (fixed cost)	$100.00

Production Costs

1. For your company, what is the cost to produce one star? _____
   (*Add the fixed costs plus the variable costs for one star.*)

2. For your company, what is the total cost to produce 100 stars? _____
   (*The variable costs × 100 plus the fixed cost.*)

3. Use the following production data for the next question.
   Company output: Company 1 = 50 stars   Company 3 = 200 stars
                     Company 2 = 100 stars   Company 4 = 750 stars

   For your company, what is the average cost for each star produced? _____
   (*Multiply the variable costs times number of stars produced. Add the fixed cost. Divide the total by the number of stars produced.*)

4. For your company, what is the price you should charge if you want to make a profit (gain) of $1.00 per star? _____

5. How did using physical capital affect the quality and cost of producing stars?
   _____
   _____

6. How does using physical capital affect your ability to produce things people want?
   _____
   _____

From *Choices and Changes in Life, School, and Work*, 5–6, © National Council on Economic Education, New York, NY

New Technologies Change How People Work

Inventions can greatly affect the number of workers needed for production as well as what they do while working. This is the story of how many inventions changed the way cotton cloth was produced.

In the 1700s, one worker spent one day cleaning one pound of cotton bolls by hand. The cleaned cotton was ready to be spun into cotton thread.

With clean cotton, hand spinners sat at spinning wheels each day to produce enough thread to start a weaving loom. Then the thread could be woven into cotton cloth.

Things began to change in 1733, when John Kay invented the flying shuttle. Now cotton thread could be woven into cloth much faster than by using a hand weaving loom.

Since workers were still cleaning cotton by hand and spinning cotton into thread using a spinning wheel, many more workers were needed to pick cotton, clean cotton, and spin cotton into thread.

Thirty years later, James Hargreaves invented the spinning jenny. This machine spun cotton into thread much faster than the hand spinning wheel. Workers who were hand spinners were no longer needed to produce cotton thread. Each worker on a spinning jenny could produce 10 times as much yarn in a given time period as a worker using a spinning wheel.

In 1785 the flying shuttle loom was improved. The improved loom was powered by rapidly moving river water. This loom could weave thread into cloth much faster. Again, weaving was faster, but there was not enough clean cotton. The price of cotton increased because there was not enough to supply those who wanted to weave it into cloth.

9-1 (continued)

New Technologies Change How People Work

In 1793, an invention by Eli Whitney solved the problem. He invented the cotton gin. "Gin" is short for engine. With the cotton gin, one worker could clean 50 pounds of cotton bolls each day.

Now cotton growers were encouraged to grow more cotton that could be changed quickly from plant to cloth. The price of cotton dropped because it took fewer workers to clean it.

Cotton could be cleaned quickly using the cotton gin.

➜ More cleaned cotton was spun into yarn using the spinning jenny.

➜ More yarn could be woven into cloth using a power loom.

These inventions changed the way people worked in the North and encouraged farmers in the South to produce more cotton.

Large cotton mills could now produce cloth to sell in the United States and in other nations.

Industrial Revolution Timeline

Invention of the flying shuttle, John Kay	1733	
	1764	Invention of the spinning jenny, James Hargreaves
Invention of the "improved" steam engine, James Watt	1765	
	1769	Invention of the spinning frame, Richard Arkwright
Signing of the Declaration of Independence	1776	
	1785	Invention of the power loom, Edmund Cartwright
Invention of the spinning mule, Samuel Crompton	1779	
	1790	First cotton mill in Pawtucket, Rhode Island, Samuel Slater and Moses Brown
Invention of the cotton gin, Eli Whitney	1793	
	1798	Introduction of interchangeable parts manufacturing, Eli Whitney
First steamboat "Clermont," Robert Fulton	1807	
	1818	Completion of the National Road from Baltimore, Maryland to Wheeling, West Virginia
Building of the textile mills in Lowell, Massachusetts	1815	
	1820	Farm productivity increases, creating a surplus of food to sell
Erie Canal opens	1825	First successful steam locomotive, Richard Trevithick
Immigration increases for factories and transportation	1820-1840	
	1836	Strike at the textile mills Lowell, Massachusetts
Massachusetts child labor law, limited to 10 hours a day	1842	

9-3

The Industrial Revolution

From hand tools and hand-made goods to machines and mass-produced goods

---

Between 1698 and 1815, the development of new machines revolutionized the way people worked in the colonies and the young United States of America. New technologies combined with new skills of workers to change production and the way people earned income.

Turning cotton or wool into cloth required a variety of resources. Steam power was first used in England to drive textile machines. Spinning machines and looms were also powered by steam.

In the United States, water replaced steam as a source of power for the mills. Mill towns grew on the rivers in the Northeast because the rivers provided a constant source of power.

New technologies reduced the cost of production, and the price of cotton went down. Eli Whitney invented the cotton gin, an inexpensive way to clean cotton. This encouraged farmers in the South to grow more cotton.

The textile factories in the Northeast states needed more workers. Many young workers left the farms and moved to the growing cities. Large numbers of young women, with fewer opportunities in farming communities, moved to towns like Lowell, Massachusetts, to earn an income in the mills.

The growing demand for cotton in the Southern states increased the demand for slave labor. The economy of the South grew. Textile mills and farmers needed a transportation system to get goods to consumers and natural resources to the businesses.

Canals, the National Road, steamboats, and railroads were the answer. Canals were dug forty feet wide and four feet deep. Horses walked alongside the canals, pulling boats filled with goods and resources for production. When the canal system was finished, the cost of moving goods and resources went down.

9-3 (continued)

The Industrial Revolution

The National Road was built, and steamboats began to move on the rivers. This revolution in transportation also included laying railroad tracks across land, connecting small and large cities.

The Industrial Revolution changed the way work was done. Production moved from homes to factories. Prices of goods decreased. Children and women worked long and tedious hours in the factories. Some workers developed diseases such as an abnormal curvature of the spine.

Work changed and lives changed as the United States became the largest manufacturer of goods in the world.

9-4

The Mill Girls

Who were the "mill girls"? They were young women, generally 15–30 years old, who worked in the large cotton factories.

Choices and Changes

To find workers for their mills in Lowell, Massachusetts, and other cities, the textile companies recruited women from New England farms and villages. These young women had few economic opportunities on the farm, and many were enticed by the prospect of monthly cash wages and room and board in a comfortable boardinghouse. Young women also liked to work in the city because of the shopping, educational, and recreational activities offered there. Most women from small villages had never had these opportunities.

Beginning in 1823, large numbers of young women moved to the growing cities. In the mills, female workers faced long hours of work and grueling working conditions. Many female textile workers saved money and became independent.

A New Way to Live and Work

Within the factory, overseers were responsible for maintaining work discipline and meeting production schedules. In the boardinghouses, curfews and strict codes of conduct were enforced.

The clanging factory bell called workers to and from the mill, constantly reminding them that their days were structured around work. Most textile workers worked for 12 to 14 hours a day and half a day on Saturdays. The mills were closed on Sundays.

Mill girls were hired for nine to ten months of the year. Many left the factories during part of the summer to work on the farms of their families.

9-4 (continued)

The Mill Girls

Life in a Boardinghouse

Most mill girls in Lowell lived in boardinghouses. These large, company-owned buildings were often run by a female keeper or a husband and wife. A typical boardinghouse consisted of four units, with 20 to 40 women living in each unit.

For most young women, life in the boardinghouse was dramatically different from life on the farm. Usually they shared a room with three other women, sleeping two to a bed. A fireplace in each room provided warmth in the colder seasons. The keeper prepared three meals a day, and the women dined together in a common room.

Women formed many new friendships with other female boarders.

Thousands of immigrants from many other countries settled in Lowell in the years after the Civil War, yet women remained a major part of the Lowell's textile workforce.

What Will You Do?

The year is 1872. You are 16 years old. You live on a farm in western Massachusetts with your father, mother, two brothers, and two sisters. Farming has been difficult for the past couple of years. Life on the farm is monotonous, and the small town you live near has little opportunity for you. On a trip to town to purchase some supplies, you notice this sign.

> **Mill Workers Wanted**
>
> **Young men and women**
> from 15 to 35 years of age
> wanted to work in the
>
> **COTTON MILLS**
> in Lowell and Chicopee, Mass.
>
> **Clean housing and meals available.**

You have at least two alternatives:

- Stay on the farm with your family for at least five more years until you are able to marry and have a farm of your own.

- Move to Lowell or Chicopee to work in the cotton mill for at least three years when you will have saved enough to marry and start a business or family.

At a family dinner, you ask your family if they think that you should go to Lowell or Chicopee, or stay on the farm. What will they say? Choose "yes" or "no" and tell why.

Yes. ☐ Why?   No. ☐ Why?
_____   _____
_____   _____
_____   _____
_____   _____

10-1

Interdependence at Work

In the spaces under **The Barn**, describe examples from the story of specialization, division of labor, and interdependence.

In the spaces under **Making the Story Quilt**, describe examples from the activity of specialization, division of labor, and interdependence.

The Barn	Making the Story Quilt
Specialization	Specialization
Division of Labor	Division of Labor
Interdependence	Interdependence

Many hands make light work.
Leroy W. Jones

11-1

My Future Career

I am dreaming of working as a _____

These are the ways in which I will work with others.

_____

_____

_____

_____

Draw a picture of yourself working with others in your future career.

12-1

Survival Means Working Together

In the early 1600s, two groups of people sailed west from England to find religious freedom and the new wealth promised by the riches of North America. The three ships of the Virginia Company sailed on May 24, 1607, landing near what would become Jamestown, Virginia.

A few years later in 1620, a single small ship, the *Mayflower*, set sail with 100 Pilgrims planning to settle north of Jamestown, but landed far from there in an area that is now Plymouth, Massachusetts.

Both of these groups planned to settle permanently in North America. They expected to take advantage of the region's wealth of resources. Both the Pilgrims on the *Mayflower* and the Jamestown settlers found that rich natural resources would not be enough to achieve their goals.

The settlers of Jamestown thought they would easily find gold and other riches. The time they spent searching for gold meant that they did not plant crops, did not build shelters, and did not do the other things that they had to do to survive. When Captain John Smith arrived at Jamestown in 1608, he found a disaster waiting to happen.

In Jamestown, seventy-three of the settlers died within the first seven months. Smith convinced the surviving colonists that if they did not work together, they would not survive. Their agreement was simple, as Captain Smith dictated, "He that will not work, shall not eat."

With this new resolve, some of the Jamestown colonists planted crops; others built houses; and some built the fences needed to protect themselves. As they learned to work together, their chances of survival increased.

After 66 days at sea, the Pilgrims signed their compact to form a government in the new area where they finally landed. They agreed to make laws ". . . for the general good of the colony, unto which we promise all due. . ."

They knew that without an agreement to work together, their chances for survival were small.

The Mayflower Compact

In the name of God, Amen. We, whose names are underwritten, the Loyal Subjects of our dread Sovereign Lord, King James, by the Grace of God, of England, France and Ireland, King, Defender of the Faith, etc.

Having undertaken for the Glory of God, and Advancement of the Christian Faith, and the Honour of our King and Country, a voyage to plant the first colony in the northern parts of Virginia; do by these presents, solemnly and mutually in the Presence of God and one of another, covenant and combine ourselves together into a civil Body Politick, for our better Ordering and Preservation, and Furtherance of the Ends aforesaid; And by Virtue hereof to enact, constitute, and frame, such just and equal Laws, Ordinances, Acts, Constitutions and Offices, from time to time, as shall be thought most meet and convenient for the General good of the Colony; unto which we promise all due submission and obedience.

In Witness whereof we have hereunto subscribed our names at Cape Cod the eleventh of November, in the Reign of our Sovereign Lord, King James of England, France and Ireland, the eighteenth, and of Scotland the fifty-fourth. Anno Domini, 1620.

In 1620, the Pilgrims on the *Mayflower* landed far from their intended destination and found themselves outside any existing social order or political rule. Understanding that they needed some order to their relationships, they signed an agreement, known as the *Mayflower Compact*.

In the compact, they agreed to govern themselves so that the group would survive. They had the good fortune to meet and befriend Native Americans who taught them the skills they needed to make the most of their resources. The Pilgrims increased their production by specializing and survived.

12-3

Working Together

You are members of a team that will produce

_____

You must write a compact about how you will work together.

The Compact

- Why will it be important for the members of the group to work together?
- What rules will you agree to follow to successfully accomplish your goal?
- What incentives are there for the group to work together?
- How will your group make decisions?
- How will you make sure that everyone works?
- How will your group share the benefits of accomplishing your goal?
- Sign the agreement.

We must indeed all hang together, or, most assuredly, we shall all hang separately.
  Benjamin Franklin, on the signing of the *Declaration of Independence*

13-1

My Goals

Goals can be things you want to own in the future. Goals can be things you want to do in the future. Goals can include your career in the future.

Directions

1. In the box below, make a list of your future goals.

2. Review your goals. Number them in order of their priority or importance to you. Number one should be the most important goal on your list.

3. Review your goals again. Put a star ☆ next to each of the goals that will be easier to achieve if you increase your human capital through more education.

4. Review your goals again. Put a check mark ✔ next to each goal that will be easier to accomplish if you learn to work with others.

5. Review your list of goals.

6. Look at all the goals you can accomplish!

My goals are:

People with goals succeed because they know where they are going.   Earl Nightingale

The Road to Success—Scorecard

Name _____		Name _____	
Starting Points	10	Starting Points	10
Turn 1		Turn 1	
Total		Total	
Turn 2		Turn 2	
Total		Total	
Turn 3		Turn 3	
Total		Total	
Turn 4		Turn 4	
Total		Total	
Turn 5		Turn 5	
Total		Total	
Turn 6		Turn 6	
Total		Total	
Turn 7		Turn 7	
Total		Total	
Turn 8		Turn 8	
Total		Total	
Turn 9		Turn 9	
Total		Total	
Turn 10		Turn 10	
Final Total		Final Total	

You don't just stumble into your future. You create your own future. — Roger Smith

Title _____   Author _____

A Web of Traits

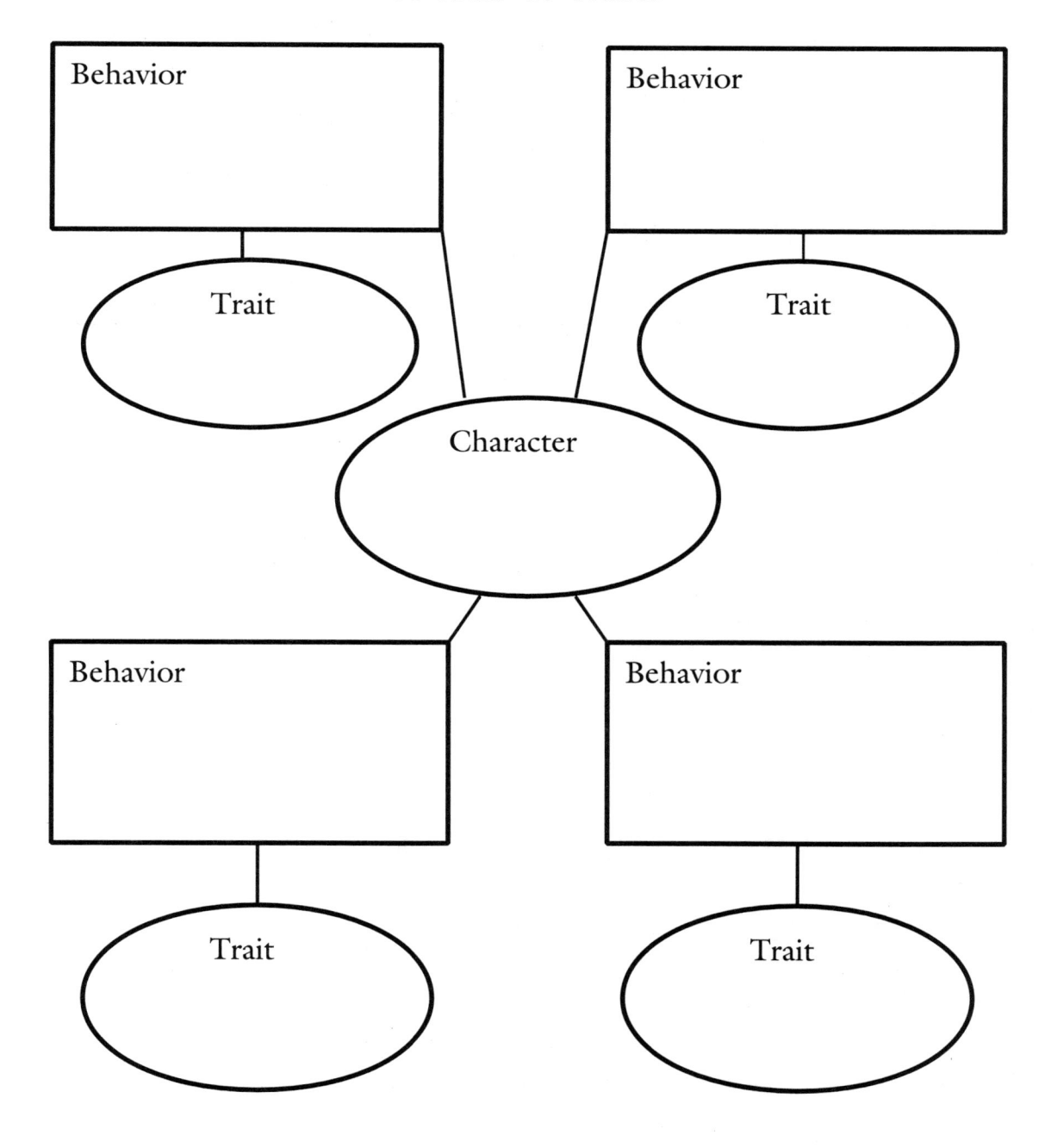

- Behavior
- Trait
- Behavior
- Trait
- Character
- Behavior
- Trait
- Behavior
- Trait

14-3

Reaching My Future Goal

My future goal is _____
_____

I can plan to accomplish my goal by _____
_____
_____

The positive incentives for accomplishing my goal are _____
_____
_____

The obstacles I may face are _____
_____
_____

To overcome the obstacles, I will _____
_____
_____

When I accomplish my goal, I _____
_____
_____

15-1

Traits for Success

Successful people have. . .

Motivation

Motivation is what encourages successful people to work hard, to get an education, and to develop the skills and knowledge they need to achieve their goals. Successful people are motivated by incentives—the positives and negatives, the benefits and costs of choices—to set goals, plan, and overcome obstacles.

Curiosity

Successful people have a desire to understand the people and the world around them. Successful people have the ability to find and use the information they need to make decisions that are in their best interests.

Problem-Solving Ability

Successful people are problem solvers. They accept the challenge of analyzing situations, determining the costs and benefits of the alternatives, and making informed choices. Successful people know how to allocate and organize resources to accomplish difficult tasks.

Persistence

Successful people have the ability to keep working on achieving a goal or solving a problem even though it is difficult. Successful people do not give up on their goals or quit just because there are obstacles in their way. They are able to identify obstacles and find ways to overcome them.

Leadership

Successful people have the ability to work with others in teams or as leaders. They can communicate with their team members and others with whom they are interdependent. Successful people can share information, compromise, and reach consensus to solve problems and accomplish goals.

It is not your aptitude, but your attitude, that determines your altitude.   Zig Zigler

A Successful Person

Book title _____

Biography of _____

Dates covered _____

What did this person accomplish? _____
_____

What obstacles did the person face? _____
_____
_____

How did the person overcome the obstacles? _____
_____
_____

How did the person's accomplishments benefit others? _____
_____
_____

What personal character traits made this person a success? _____
_____
_____

UNIT FIVE ASSESSMENT

Deborah Sampson: A Success Story

Deborah Sampson was born in Plympton, Massachusetts, on December 17, 1760. When she was 10 years old, she became an indentured servant to the household of Jeremiah Thomas in Middleborough. There she helped with the housework and worked in the fields.

In the fields, Deborah worked alongside Mr. Thomas' 10 sons, learning many new skills. While she received no formal education in her early years, as was the custom of the times, she learned much from the 10 boys as they returned from school each day.

In later years, she worked in the fields throughout the spring, summer, and fall, developing her physical strength. She was taller and much stronger than most women of that time. During the winter, with less physical work to do, she attended school. When her nine-year indenture ended in 1779, she had learned enough to be hired as a teacher at a Middleborough public school.

Deborah also worked spinning and weaving cloth at Sproats Tavern, where she heard many tales of the battles of the Revolutionary War and the heroic exploits of some local young men. These stories filled her with a sense of adventure and responsibility to others.

One day in the spring of 1782, a tall, thin young man named Robert Shurtliff arrived at the muster station and volunteered to join the Revolutionary Army. No one knew that this young patriot was a woman, Deborah Sampson. To achieve her goal, she had learned how to walk, talk, and act like a man. The Revolutionary Army did not require physical examinations.

At the Battle of Tarrytown, she suffered a head wound and was hit in the leg by a musket ball. She treated the leg injury herself in order to prevent discovery of her true gender. Her true identity was not discovered until she was hospitalized with a fever. The doctor kept her secret and helped to make arrangements to end her military service. Private Shurtliff was honorably discharged from the army October 23, 1783.

Deborah returned to Plympton, but soon left again because of her mother's disapproval of her military service. She went to the home of an aunt in a nearby town where she again dressed as a man so that she could find the work she wanted.

She stopped posing as a man only when she met Benjamin Gannett, whom she later married. Deborah and Benjamin lived a simple life, often borrowing money from acquaintances to get by. One acquaintance, Paul Revere, helped to arrange a small military pension for Deborah in recognition of her heroic war service.

Deborah Sampson Gannett died on April 29, 1827, in Sharon, Massachusetts. As a legacy of her spirit, her family coat of arms carries the motto, "Disgrace Is Worse Than Death."

UNIT FIVE ASSESSMENT (continued)

Deborah Sampson: A Success Story

After reading the biographical sketch about American Revolutionary War hero Deborah Sampson, answer the following questions about her success story.

1. What was Deborah Sampson's goal?

   _____
   _____

2. What obstacles did she have to overcome?

   _____
   _____
   _____

3. How did she plan to achieve her goal?

   _____
   _____
   _____

4. What personal character traits and human capital did she have that helped her to achieve her goal?

   _____
   _____
   _____
   _____
   _____

UNIT FIVE HOME AND COMMUNITY CONNECTION

Overcoming Obstacles and Achieving A Family Goal

The goal we set is _____

_____

We plan to accomplish our goal by _____

_____

_____

The positive incentives for accomplishing our goal are _____

_____

_____

The obstacles we will face are _____

_____

_____

We will overcome the obstacles by _____

_____

_____

When we accomplish our goal, we _____

_____

_____